MW00512571

SWING TRADING
STRATEGIES

Learn How To Trade, Predicting trends And Dominating The
Market. Master Tips And Secrets And Improve your Knowledge
In Trading Investing With Options, Futures And Stocks

MARK KRATTER

content within this book has been derived from various sources. Please consult a licensed professional before attempting any techniques outlined in this book.

By reading this document, the reader agrees that under no circumstances is the author responsible for any losses, direct or indirect, which are incurred as a result of the use of information contained within this document, including, but not limited to, errors, omissions, or inaccuracies.

Table of Contents

Introduction 7

Chapter 1 - Moving Averages 16

Chapter 2 - Strategies and Techniques of Swing Trade 26

Chapter 3 - Fibonacci Retracement Trading Strategy 35

Chapter 4 - Breakout & Breakdown trading 43

Chapter 5 - Planning Your Trade 50

Chapter 6 - Daily Routine of a Swing Trader 58

Chapter 7 - Entry and Exit Strategies for Traders 68

Chapter 8 - Protecting Your Capital and Managing Your Money
.... 72

Conclusion 81

Introduction

What Most People Do

When it comes to the stock market and traders, most individuals are looking for the high-volume trades, with fluctuating prices. They get in, make a profit, and get out to find the next big profit.

Final Thoughts

The shares are first released from a company to gain investment funds. The shares are then traded as a way to garner dividends and profit from the up and downtrends in the market. The market also allows you to invest in various exchanges around the world, as long as your broker provides access. Most people trade in their country's stock market or the largest in their region like the Japan Stock Exchange, London Stock Exchange, and NYSE.

Swing trading is popular amongst many investors. It can be applied to a wide array of financial instruments including currencies, futures, stocks, and options. Each of these instruments has its own advantages and disadvantages. It is the only style that utilizes both long-term as well as day trading strategies.

Swing trading is often used by new as well as experienced traders. It carries several benefits that are not easy to ignore. It basically entails monitoring price movements or 'swings' then seeking to make a profit from these swings. To do this, you must enter and exit positions at the right time. Swing trading is always less concerned about the fundamental aspects of financial instruments since it is a relatively short-term form of trading.

Since swing trading entails making a profit, it is important to choose the right financial instruments to trade. Essentially, there are numerous factors you need to establish before settling on a particular instrument to swing trade. Some of these factors include:

Liquidity of the instrument. Liquidity is the ease with which traders sell and purchase certain financial instruments on the swing market. As a swing trader, you should focus on instruments that feature high liquidity since these are easy to buy and sell.

Compatibility with rule-based systems. Most swing traders always use systems that are rule-based to carry out their trades. Such systems allow traders to create more reliable trading signals. As you select a financial instrument, ensure that you can use it on such platforms.

The volatility of the instrument. Volatility is the rate at which the cost or value of particular security changes. This can either be a rise or decline in the price. Highly volatile securities are often easier to sell than those with low volatility. However, these are also associated with multiple risk levels. Most long-term investors often avoid stocks that bear large price swings. On the other hand, for swing and day traders, such a swing is what causes profits to be realized. You can benefit from upward and downward price swings alike.

Alignment to market trends. The swing market will always assume a bearish or bullish state. It is important to identify financial securities that are capable of moving with these trends. Trading software can assist you in filtering the kind of stocks available for trading to only those that are aligned with the current market trend.

Transaction costs. Different financial instruments feature different trading costs. If you have limited capital, you will need to choose an instrument that requires less cash to trade. Several financial instruments always require very little capital to trade. These include brokerage fees and commissions.

Information availability. Some financial instruments are popular than others. The availability of information is necessary in case you need to learn about a strategy or skill required to trade a particular stock. For example, if you do not have access to financial news updates relating to a certain financial instrument, it becomes difficult for you to estimate when the prices may change. Therefore, as you choose a financial instrument, make sure that its information is freely accessible.

Subject to technical analysis. Some financial instruments work best with technical analysis while others do not. As you make your choice, ensure that the instrument you select is easy to analyze using technical indicators and patterns. Most swing traders use technical indicators because they are simple, systematic, and easy to use. When applied correctly, technical analysis generates the right signals that you can use to enter and exit the swing market.

Besides the few points above, you also need to consider the level of risk associated with the instrument as well as the current market conditions where the instrument can be traded. Because swing trading favors a number of securities, it is easy for you to diversify your investments in a manner that reduces the risks associated with the traded.

Swing Trading Stocks

Stocks are financial securities that indicate ownership of a certain company and its assets. Trading in stocks can get a bit confusing if you do not understand the various types available on the market today. If you are a novice swing trader, mastering this can take you a lot of time. However, for professional stock traders is no big deal. To trade in stocks, you must specify the level of risk you are ready to tolerate and the amount of time you would like to leave positions open.

There are generally two major types of stocks—preferred stocks and common stocks. Commons stocks are those that are freely available to the public for trading. Most of the stocks available on the market today are of this form. They give you ownership of the company and part of the profits. These are often associated with high profits than other categories of financial instruments.

Preferred stocks, on the other hand, give you some level of right over a company but not the right to vote. The guidelines associated with preferred stocks always vary from one company to another. In case the company decides to go liquid, owners of preferred stocks are often paid off their share costs before those holding common stocks receive their payment.

Stocks can also be customized depending on certain classes. For instance, there are blue-chip stocks which represent shares from large companies that keep experiencing tremendous growth. Traders always prefer such stocks over other types because the returns are guaranteed. There are also speculative stocks that represent shares from organizations with a very undefined financial history. Such stocks feature high levels of risk since their stability is questionable. Nevertheless, the stocks always bear high-profit capabilities and some traders ignore the risk associated with them.

With growth stocks, the company listing them always has the potential for receiving high returns in form of earnings. Such companies reinvest their earnings back into the business for it to grow. They also pay some dividends to stock owners depending on the number of shares invested. Value stocks are often undervalued but carry great profit potential. Investors always purchase such stocks with the hope that the price will eventually be revised to a fair one in the future. Lastly, penny stocks feature very low prices, low volatility, and high risk. These are often avoided by most people because they rarely generate any income.

When trading stocks, you should look for those that have high-profit potential and high-risk tolerance. When choosing the right stocks to trade in, be sure to check their volume levels. Most swing traders always choose stocks that are highly liquid. This is because it is easier to close positions associated with high volume stocks faster. Since swing trading requires that you close positions soon enough to realize a profit, it is essential that you have liquidity of stock in mind when seeking the right one for the trade. Such stocks also feature lower bid-ask spreads that are favorable for swing trading.

Another aspect you need to have in mind when trading in stocks is the availability of the stock with market makers. These are individuals who hold certain stocks for some time to increase their liquidity and balance the market. Most of them are always paid a small amount for holding the shares. As a swing trader, your focus should be getting such stocks since this will ensure that you are dealing with an instrument that will remain on demand during the entire trading period.

When swing trading a particular stock, check how it correlates with market indices and other categories of stocks. This is because some stocks may seem to have the right trading features, but these end up swinging against the market direction. If you trade in these stocks, you will end up losing a good percentage of your capital. You need to focus on stocks that are volatile enough to cause a price swing. Swing trading becomes irrelevant when you apply the style on stocks whose prices are not moving.

As you get the right stock for swing trading, you want to find out if there are any upcoming activities and events that may affect the stock prices significantly. Such events may be things like the release of a new product, or an upcoming earning for the company. Here are a few quick tips that you can use to swing trading stocks:

- Use both short-term and long-term charts as well as time frames.
- Enter the market as soon as price trends start and not at the end of it.
- Use more than one indicator to analyze the market.
- Align your swings with the market direction.
- Have a trading plan before you start swing trading.
- Master all the aspects of swing trading.
- Check out for daily news on the underlying company and industry before entering positions. Also, be mindful of general market news such as economic and political news as these can impact stock prices drastically.

- Go long when the market is strong, and short when the market is weak.
- Monitor trends in the market prices and trade in relation to the trend.

Chapter 1 - Moving Averages

Moving averages are another very popular and relatively simple trading tool that can be used by a swing trader. They can assist you in getting a good entry on a stock and further help you to stay in a position to take advantage of a long-term trend. They can also provide a good signal for when you should make an exit.

Moving averages come in 2 primary types: simple and exponential. Both of these moving averages can be calculated using different periods of time. The longer the time period used, the more likely the average will lag behind a stock price in an uptrend or downtrend. Let's start by looking at the difference between the simple and exponential moving averages, and then look at different time periods, and then, finally, consider how best to use them with your swing trading strategies.

Simple vs. Exponential Moving Averages

The difference between the simple moving average (SMA) and the exponential moving average (EMA) can be significant, and your choice of which one you choose to use can make an impact on your trading. An SMA is calculated by starting with a period of time. Let's use 20 days as an example. You take the closing price for each of the past 20 days, add these price numbers together, and then divide by 20. This gives you the average price for those 20 days.

The next day you repeat the same process with the new set of numbers: the oldest day from your past calculation gets dropped out because it is no longer in your 20-day range and the most recent closing price replaces it. As each day passes, you calculate a new 20-day SMA number that you can plot on a graph against the time. For the 50-day and the 200-day SMAs, you go through the same process with the corresponding number of days.

If the stock price you are plotting is constantly moving down, then the moving average prices get dragged lower as well. This gives you a trendline that you can monitor for trend changes. In our example, if the price reverses and starts to move higher, then the stock price will eventually cross the moving average, which has been lagging behind the current price movement. This cross provides a possible indicator of a change in sentiment.

Figure 8.5 shows a plot of Micron Technology, Inc. (MU) trending lower with the moving averages following the price down until it starts to reverse. On August 14th, MU's price crosses over the 20-day SMA. This is a sign of a possible change in investor sentiment with a new uptrend beginning. In our MU example, the price consolidates (churns sideways) for almost 2 weeks until the price starts to break above the 50-day SMA. After this event, the price trend change is clearly established and MU's stock price moves higher.

The chart of MU also shows how for a number of times the 20-day SMA acts as a support as the stock moves higher with waves of buying and selling. This illustrates how moving averages can be used to get a good entry in a trade and also to keep you in the trade in order to maximize profits.

The exponential moving average calculation is a little more complicated so I will not provide an explanation of it in this book. The formulas used are readily available on the Internet. The important thing to know when comparing the 2 different moving averages is that the EMA is more sensitive to recent changes in the price of the stock. This means that the EMA will react more quickly and, depending upon the situation, may or may not be good.

Because the EMA reacts faster when the price changes direction, it can provide an earlier signal of a possible change in trend. But, especially during times of higher volatility, this quicker reaction can also give the wrong signal. Stocks move in waves regardless of what direction they are moving: up, down or sideways. If a stock in a downtrend starts to bounce higher after a wave of selling, the EMA could start pointing up and potentially send a signal that there is an overall change in direction of the stock's price. This may not be the case if it is just a temporary bounce higher before continuing on a downtrend. Therefore, this early indicator can result in a false trend change signal.

Because the SMA moves more slowly, it can keep you in a winning trade longer by smoothing out the inevitable bounces or pullbacks that normally occur during a long-term trend. Conversely, this slower-moving trend line may also keep you in a trade when the trend has actually changed, so you may have to use other tools or fundamental analysis to decide if this trend is changing to the other direction. You will more often use the SMA when you are in your trades for longer durations and you are thus wanting to stay with a trend for as long as possible.

Due to the different levels of sensitivity between the 2 types of moving averages, you should consider adjusting which one to use based on the particular market environment. In volatile markets, where prices are bouncing up and down, an SMA may be a better tool. In less volatile market conditions, you would consider using the EMA to get earlier entry signals on trend changes.

Referring to Figure 8.6, you can see the difference between using the 20-day SMA versus the 20-day EMA. You'll notice that the EMA gives a slightly earlier signal as the MU price first crosses the faster reacting, moving average. In this case, you may have got a slightly lower entry price on the trade, however, given the great run on MU it would not have made a big difference in your total return on the trade.

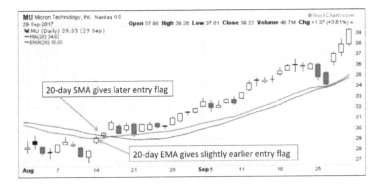

Moving Average Time Periods

As a swing trader using moving average tools, you will need to consider what periods of time you want to use that give the best signals for your trading style. The first thing you should do is to stay with some of the periods that are commonly used by traders and computers. These moving averages work as technical indicators because they are, in effect, self-fulfilling prophecies. Many other traders and machines are looking at the same indicators and they work in part because of that fact.

The shorter the number of days used to calculate the moving average, the sooner you will see a change in direction because the short time periods more strongly reflect current price action. Like the EMA, these shorter time frames can be good in identifying a shift in sentiment between the buyers and sellers, but they can also give false signals by reflecting the waves of buying and selling that occur within the typical wave action movements of a stock's price.

The most common periods used by swing traders are 20-day, 50-day and 200-day SMAs. Because traders are watching price movements in relation to these averages, they usually offer areas of support and resistance. The 200-day SMA is highly revered and normally provides the strongest level of support when a stock is selling off and the strongest level of resistance when a stock is starting to move higher from a low.

Traders also use the percentage of stocks in the market that are trading above their 200-day average as a gauge to determine the overall health of the stock market. The higher the percentage of stocks above their 200-day SMA, the more the overall market is biased to trending higher, therefore, the better trades for a swing trader may be long trades versus going short.

Below are some further thoughts to consider in developing your strategies related to using moving averages when swing trading:

- The 20-day SMA is a good tool to use for a short-term swing trade. In a trending stock, the price action will often respect this level and it will also quickly identify a shift in sentiment and thus a reversal in trend.

- The 20-day EMA is a faster-reacting tool that can be used for short-term swing trades. It can get you into a trade earlier but in more volatile markets, it can also give you a false trend reversal signal.

- The 50-day SMA is also a popular gauge for a longer-term swing trade and it will allow you to ride a potentially profitable trade longer in order to make additional gains. It is a good intermediate balance between the shorter 20-day and the longer 200-day SMAs.

- The 200-day SMA represents almost 1 year of past price action (there are about 250 trading days in a year). In a down trending stock, this SMA may provide significant support and therefore be a good entry for a long position due to it being a very popular level for traders. The risk on this sort of trade is when the price finds a support level just below the 200-day SMA and the trader is then stopped out.

The Golden Cross and the Death Cross

One other way to use moving averages to determine a directional price change is to watch for what traders refer to as a "golden cross" or a "death cross." This indicator uses the 50-day and 200-day

SMAs. For example, let's consider a stock that has been in a long-term downtrend. Due to this trend, the 50-day moving average is creating a line that is below the 200-day SMA line. A golden cross signal on this stock will occur when the 50-day SMA crosses the 200-day moving average from below to above. When this happens, it is an indication that the negative sentiment is possibly changing with the downtrend in price shifting to an uptrend. This cross happens because the 50-day SMA is reflecting more current price action while the 200-day SMA is lagging further behind, reflecting prices that are further in the past.

The death cross is the opposite of the golden cross. It occurs when a stock is in a general uptrend and the price action starts to trend lower. Once again, the faster-reacting 50-day SMA starts to turn down faster than the slower reacting 200-day SMA and they eventually cross. The 50-day SMA crosses from above the 200-day SMA to below it, showing a change in sentiment and stock price direction.

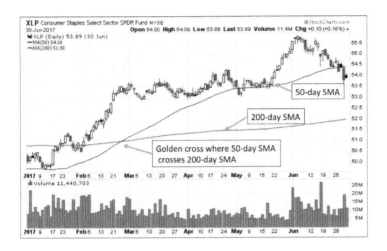

XLP Consumer Staples Select Sector SPDR Fund NYSE ⓦStockCharts.com
30-Jun-2017   Open 54.00 High 54.09 Low 53.88 Last 53.89 Volume 11.4M Chg +0.10 (+0.18%) ▲
MXLP (Daily) 53.89 (30 Jun)
—MA(50) 54.38
—MA(200) 51.90

50-day SMA

200-day SMA

Golden cross where 50-day SMA
crosses 200-day SMA

Moving Averages in Range-Bound Stocks and Markets

As a swing trader, you need to be aware that SMA and EMA tools do not work well in markets or in stocks that are trading in a limited range (where the price makes relatively small moves between support and resistance). This type of market or stock is referred to as being "range-bound," and the price action is commonly referred to as "churning." In these range-bound trading cases, all of the different time period SMA and EMA lines ripple sideways between levels of support and resistance. The price action does not respect these lines; therefore, these tools are most effective when trends are occurring: either higher or lower.

24

Chapter 2 - Strategies and Techniques of Swing Trade

Swing trading usually involves making small profits or gains from a certain investment for short periods by focusing on the changing trends. The period here is usually dependent on whether the trade remains profitable or not; it may last from one day to several weeks. The individuals usually identify instruments that have short term price momentum through an exhaustive technical analysis of the market trend and patterns. This identification, however, requires various techniques and strategies. This article explains in-depth some of these techniques and strategies that will be of much essence, specifically to the beginners.

Deciding on the choice of the Right Market. It becomes very challenging for individuals to make decisions on whether or not to join the market, especially in cases where there are two market extremes (the bear or bull market). It is, therefore, advisable to develop a strategy that will be based on the longer-term trend. You should be patient enough to wait for the market prices to go down below the Support, then after a price rejection usually just close to the Support, join the market and set up your stop loss below the candle low, then be keen to harness all the profits before Resistance. By this, in most circumstances, you are always assured of collecting gains rather than losses. When one joins the market

26

when the stocks are high, you are at a greater risk of accumulating losses instead of gains. The idea here is to enter the market after prices have fallen and exit when the price pressures tend to step up.

You could decide on what stocks or instruments to swing trade with. It is usually advisable to settle for stocks that have heavy uplifting. This refers to the large capital stocks that usually have the tendency to go through extreme highs and lows over a considerable length of time. These enable you to understand the trend and patterns more easily and, more so, enjoy the profits for considerable lengths before the prices break down. Identifying the right stock to swing trade with is a fundamental factor in your success when swing trading. In most circumstances, as a trader, you will be tempted to just make a trade without checking the right stock features. This may end up being your downfall despite having the best trading pattern or strategy. That's why stock screeners are usually advisable while doing your investment research.

Another strategy towards success in swing trading is to have a correct and straightforward mental discipline as far as sticking to your strategies and plans is concerned. This usually calls for mental toughness and the quality of being decisive and sticking to your initial plans. Combating fear and making decisions based on these eons are usually high risk and getting too personal with one's losses as well as a discouraging factor that can actually drive you out of the market and make you beat yourself always due to that bad trade.

Like any other business, one should persevere the losses and understand that at one point in time, if they layout correct strategies, then they will yield enormous profits. Always create a positive mental attitude towards your trade. Loses made should be regarded as learned mistakes that one should fight hard not to repeat. They should actually be regarded as learning opportunities to better one's trade.

Something you should uphold is the counter trending strategy. This usually assumes that the current trend will actually reverse in time. It, however, calls for many disciplines, especially in cases where one has to admit that they have made the wrong strategy and are supposed to draw a line over the trading failure to which you will encounter very large losses. When you recognize this trading pattern and trend, you try to join in when you anticipate that there will be a reversion, especially after the upstream. This creates the perception that consecutively, the swing will have to change direction at some point in time. Having this in mind, you should be sharp to realize the unforeseen reversal. To assess the chances of a reversal, one can use the Arms Index as well as the Put/Cut Ratio.

Being up to date with the current News is another core strategy; these as you are aware of the basis under which market prices fluctuate. Being up to date with this news as well as the new developments in the market places one in a good position to make sound decisions concerning when to and not to trade. You should always ensure that you have properly equipped yourself with the quickest and most reliable form of media that will enable you to get wind of any critical issue that may directly or indirectly affect the market prices. Some of the issues to be on the lookout for include: The security and stability of various countries and states, the growth of various business sectors, the tone of a market, e.g., inflation levels, etc. This know-how enables one to find special opportunities that, despite having high risks, have high returns in case one type of research on them exhaustively.

You should always ensure that you always enter the market at the start of the trade, not when it is almost ending. This gives you a better opportunity to accrue higher profits due to the fact that the profit ladder in this position may be high and consistent as compared to when the trade is ending. In such situations, you do not risk losing your profits insignificantly. The chances of accruing many profits when the trade is ending are also very minimal, and the profits are also wanting, especially when compared to the losses that one can make.

Another great strategy is ensuring that you following keenly on the trend or wave of a particular stock. Identify one particular trend that follows the 50-period Moving Average. The 50 MA is usually preferred since it is used worldwide by traders hence creating the basis that its prophecy may, to some extent, fulfill the desired result. Moreover, in most circumstances, the 50 MA seems to follow in line with past Resistant and Support. If, at any instance, the markets start approaching the moving average, then be patient enough to wait for the bullish price rejection, go to the next candle, and exit the market before the next swing high.

Take advantage of the scalping strategy. This is usually a type of trading strategy that is aimed at acquiring very small profits. It is based on the fact that small moves in stocks can easily be achieved as compared to larger ones. Most of the traders who practice this strategy usually place anywhere from 10 to a few hundred. They, however, accrue considerable amounts of profits if at all, they are able to employ a strict exit strategy.

Another swing trading strategy that you should uphold is the MACD crossover. It is categorized as one of the most popular indicators used by forex in determining trend direction. It consists of two lines that move at different rates (fast and slow) buy and sell signals are obtained in case the two lines meet or crossover. The fast-moving form, in this case, would usually represent the MACD line and the slow-moving line is the signal line. Where the MACD line makes across through the signal line on the upper side, then it indicates an uptrend, and hence you look forward to buying. However, when the MACD line makes a crossover the signal line in the lower side, then it indicates a downstream, and hence you look forward to selling. The MACD crossover is known to work effectively in the case of a strong trending market. This strategy can yield maximum profits as a result, not forgetting that it is the simplest method of trading with minimal complications.

Another popular strategy is the use of simple moving averages. You can calculate the constantly changing averages of a single day from say 10 days and another for say 20 days; you can then join the averages to form a smooth curve that will represent the price changes. When the simple averages cross on either side of the stock chart, then it would mean a tentative buy or sell depending on the side they cross. This will enable you to make sound decisions on when or whether to buy or sell. Your moves will always be calculated, hence lowering the chances of making constant losses.

Another most commonly used strategy is the Fibonacci retracement. The term Fibonacci retracement is used to refer to areas of Support and Resistance. It has horizontal lines with percentages that enable the identification of the position of Support and Resistance levels. You can use Fibonacci retracement to place and determine the stop loss, set the price targets, or even the entry orders. You may decide to buy when the stock retraces to say 68.1% and then bounces back at the Fibonacci level. Moreover, you may set up the stop loss to 78.6% or rather where the move primarily started.

Another technique is the use of a T-line strategy, you can identify a T-line diagram and then use it to make your decisions as well as conclusions, in case your trade closes above the T-line then expect that the price will continue to rise and if the trade closes below the T-line then expect that the price may continue to decrease. This is, however, based on probability, and the result must not be rigid.

Another strategy that you would consider giving special considerations is making sure you understand the company that you are dealing with, that you understand all the basic fundamentals of a stock, get to know the management of that company. Most of the swing traders tend not to show any concern for this, and they forget that the particulars of that company in case there are any emerging issues that affect them, then there will be considerable fluctuations in the prices of the stock.

In the case where one feels opposed to the interpretation of the traditional bar charts, then you can opt to use the Japanese candlesticks as they are very easy to understand and interpret. With the information you derive from the interpretation of these bar charts, e.g., the intensity of the buying and selling pressure, you can be in a position to make relevant decisions on the kind of investment to indulge yourself in. Be it buying or selling.

Applying the rubber band trade technique, as per this strategy, always yearn as much as possible to buy the bottoms and pick the top. It is, however, not a smooth position to be in as far as swing trading is concerned. Nonetheless, if you are patient enough to wait for a time when a solid technical setup has been established, and when the trend can be regarded as somehow predictable. Then you can identify entry points that will be extremely rewarding and hence alienate yourself from the pain of having to suffer losses from the trade. Above all, the best strategy is not that which you acquire from books, but it is that which you practice, acquire through critical analysis, practice on it, and found exciting and working best for you.

Chapter 3 - Fibonacci Retracement Trading Strategy

Fibonacci might not be a strange word to you. If you have studied mathematics on a slightly deeper level, you are likely to have heard of the word. In mathematics, the meaning ascribed to Fibonacci is not complex. It simply means the sequence of integers where each is the sum of the two numbers that precede it. When it comes to technical analysis, the meaning is not so farfetched. The Fibonacci retracement levels are levels created by making use of two points which are extreme and are characteristically on a major swing high and swing low. These points are taken and divided through the use of vertical distance by ratios which we refer to as Fibonacci ratios. They are 23.6%, 38.2%, 50%, 61.8% and 100%.

How Does Fibonacci Retracement Work?

The Fibonacci retracement can be carried out in a number of steps. First, the recent swings are located. These swings are the highs and lows on the chart. The highs and lows on the charts must be found, identified, and marked. When they are found, a Fibonacci indicator is drawn between the high and low. A trend can then be formed. The aim is to trade with the trend as a guideline. When one notices an uptrend or new highs, the first test of the Fibonacci retracement strategy can be entered on. This means entering on the support level which you have drawn between the latest and most recent high and low.

What Is the Fibonacci Retracement Used For?

The whole reason this strategy was enacted was to help traders to point out support and resistance levels. The support level is the level at which prices drop so that sellers are unwilling to sell due to the high losses they would make and buyers want to buy since prices are down. This brings prices up. Resistance levels are the points where the price peaks so that sellers can make a great profit and so they try to sell and since the prices are so high, less buyers buy which drives the price down.

Why Does Fibonacci Retracement Work?

Fibonacci retracement works for a single major reason. The reason is that patterns occur naturally and Fibonacci is all about patterns. In fact, one could argue rightly that technical analysis depends on the belief that patterns and trends occur and reoccur. When a trader or analyst is able to identify a Fibonacci retracement level on a higher timeframe, he can be assured that he is not the only one who identified it. Several traders would have done so too and gone ahead to place buy and sell orders that revolve around those levels.

Fibonacci retracement levels follow the support and resistance strategy as well. Arguably, the most important Fibonacci retracements are 38.2% the 50% and the 61.8%.

Stocks usually follow trends by retracing a certain pattern percentage within an identified trend before it reverses again. When the Fibonacci levels are plotted, it can help traded identify possible reversals. If a trader can identify reversals, he can know the right times to exit and enter the market thus making the most profit he can. When a trader plots 23.6%, 38.2% and 61.8% on a stock chart, these reversal points are made visible.

Fibonacci Retracement Mistakes to Avoid

Fibonacci retracement may not be extremely uncomplicated, but that is not to say it is totally easy either. When it is being used, there are several mistakes that people make. When these mistakes are made, the result is a wrong analysis. When mistakes are made on wrong analysis, wrong trade decisions are made and that equals losses.

Fibonacci retracements are important. Reversal points are important and so if you are going to trade, you will definitely need them. This is why it is important that you understand the way it should be used rightly and avoid making mistakes. If Fibonacci retracement is used wrongly, it will equal to traders getting wrong points of entry, and losses upon losses.

Here are some mistakes that are commonly made by those who use Fibonacci retracement. These mistakes are quite common and not only rookies make them. However, now that you know them, you won't make them.

Do not mix the reference points.

The reference points are what give you the right analysis when making use of the Fibonacci retracement strategy of trade. The reference points must be consistent if you are to get proper and right answers. Think of it as a math equation. Even if you do know the right formulae and how to perform mathematical functions properly, you'd fail without the right question being answered. If you are to reference the lowest price in a trend and if you are doing it through the body of a candle or the close of a session, the best high price which you can get would be available in the body of the candle and located at the top of the trend. Think body of a candle body to a candle body and wick to wick.

If you were to mix these reference points, that is, if you were to go to the wick of the candle when you were to use the body of the candle, that is an incorrect reference point and it will result in wrong answers. You should know that as a stock trader, you will need to know how to make use of the Fibonacci without mistakes. When making use of it, special attention to be paid as mistakes cannot afford to be made. Fibonacci encourages you to keep the bigger picture in mind. Even when measuring significant moves and pullbacks, keep the bigger view in mind.

38

Do not look only at short-term trades

As a new trader, it is not easy to keep a bigger view in mind. You are relatively new and you need a particular value to predict a particular outcome. However, one of the best ways to do this is to keep the bigger picture in mind. The Fibonacci strategy is not one that focuses on only a short period. Being too narrow will block out important facts for you. When you look at only the short term aspect, you will find that you see less than you would if you viewed it on a wider scale. There are various steps you would take on long-term that you wouldn't on short-term. This becomes a problem. Often trends deceive if one doesn't look clearly. Even if you are using a technical analysis tool that is not equipped to handle reversals, it is much better to still have the bigger picture in mind in the worst case, manually. When you do this, you will see bigger opportunities and get better at avoiding traps.

Do not make use of only Fibonacci

Personally, I would never advise anyone to make use of only one analysis strategy. It is highly dangerous. Sure, it may work out fine, but what about the day it isn't. At best you'd lose 1% with a tight stop and it could be much more. Fibonacci is reliable, yes. But even the most reliable things need to be confirmed. Remember that confirming is better than regretting. If you make use of technical tools such as Moving average convergence divergence and price action itself, you'll have a higher chance and more confidence to stake up to 1 or 2 percent. I find it easier on my peace of mind to do a thorough check before picking a position.

Don't Use Fibonacci Over Short Intervals

If you make use of Fibonacci over a short interval, you will find it almost ineffective. This strategy needs to analyze long periods in order to give you what it is that you need/want. This is simply because the markets pose a lot of volatility. Due to the nature of Fibonacci, if there is not enough material included, you will find it rather ineffective.

Day trading in the foreign exchange market is exciting, but there is a lot of volatility. Volatility can cause support and resistance levels to be distorted. This will make making decisions hard and difficult to make. There are times where spikes and even whipsaws will make appearances. This can make it quite hard to figure out the best places to place stop-loss orders or sell orders.

However, this can be conquered through the simple use of more data. When you look at things from a larger angle, it becomes harder to go wrong as the data comes from a larger frame. Whatever will happen would have happened or at least shown signs of happening so that it can be predicted and taken advantage of.

The Fibonacci strategy is not as confusing as it may sound. However, you need to know what you are doing. Secondly, you need to give yourself time. When you give yourself time, you will get better at using and practicing it thereby making it harder for you to make mistakes. If it seems hard to understand or learn, don't let it put you off. There are lots of practical ways to learn it because, after a theoretical explanation like this one, a practical one is needed. Get as much material as you can and be encouraged.

Chapter 4 - Breakout & Breakdown trading

Break out trading and breakdown trading is typically what most traders look to trade when starting out. With this type of trading, one needs to be super disciplined in the approach you are taking. Having exact breakout and breakdown levels so you know when you need to get out of the trade and stops even if the stop is a mental one will keep you on the profitable side of trading. With this type of trading, taking quick profits is the name of the game and going in with a larger than average size will help the profits add up quickly. Although most beginners look to this type of trading starting out, most if not all traders eventually blow up accounts trading this strategy for a very simple reason: No discipline. This type of trading can be very profitable if the discipline is there. Having the exact entry and exit points are key in determining if you are going to be a profitable trader. This strategy typically works best if you have done your homework and are comfortable with the subject of support and resistance areas and are quick in reading the chart in determining which way the stock is going. Being reactionary works best with this trading style, let the area of support or resistance break before you buy or sell short and immediately have an area in which you get out to protect your account. Typically, if a breakout does not work, you will know immediately. A few steps to help you stay on the right side of the trade.

Step 1 – Identify why you think the stock/ticker will break out (Find the catalyst).

Step 2 – Draw support and resistance areas on the chart (Premarket information should be enabled on your platform).

Step 3 – Determine which way the stock/ticker is trending. If trending up, you are looking at a past area on the chart for resistance to break and a series of higher lows and higher highs into that break out point. The more times the breakout area is reached and not broken the better, the follow through on the trade once the area has broken will be more substantial. If trending down you are looking at a support area to break and a series of lower lows and lower highs into that breakpoint. The same thing applies here as well in terms of how many times the support area is touched but not broken.

Step 4 – Identify your stop points for the trade. This is one of the most important steps here. Not identifying your stop points will ensure your trading career is short. Having a plan when trading is crucial towards your profitability as a trader and will give you the discipline needed to succeed. No plan, no success–simple as that.

Step 5 – Once you have identified the general direction of the stock/ticker, figured out your stop points next it is time to decide the position size of the trade based on how much you are willing to risk.

Step 6 – After all these things have been identified, next is to enter the trade based on the trend of the stock.

I know it may seem like a lot of things you have to consider before you enter a trade, this is to make sure that you enter the trade with an entry plan as well as an exit plan to protect your account in case there is the breakout fails to follow through.

Now that we went over the reasons for getting into a trade and how to judge and what to do when getting into a trade, let's go over the specific things when looking for breakouts and breakdowns.

Breakouts

When I am trading breakouts, I am looking for specific types of resistance levels here. The resistance levels that I am looking for are levels that have been tested more than once and seen some significant retrace of the current up move. Once that level has been tested a few times I follow the steps above to determine where I need to get in and how much I am willing to risk based on the stop area. See the Chart below–KONE as of 7/21/2016.

Breakdowns

Some of my favorite trades here, when trading breakdowns the move typically happens quickly because of human psychology. Fear is a stronger emotion than greed, so when you are trading to the downside you need to be extremely disciplined because if the breakdown doesn't happen the ticker will turn around almost immediately and you'll be down 25 or 30 cents within a second. Identifying your stop out area first here is crucial. When the support area is identified, take a step back and look at the overall trend to make sure you see the pattern that you are seeing instead of an intermediate low in an uptrend which is what newbie traders tend to do and have large losses in trading the downside. Trading the downside is harder than trading the upside or breakout. To be on the safe side, let the support area break here and then let it retest the area and continue in the downtrend you were anticipating. See the example below.

In the above chart, you can see the areas that you need to pay attention to when trading to the downside. You see the first highs around the $4.70s range this is the initial high here. Then the low was put in and the past high was broken. The low area is where a lot of traders tend to get trapped thinking that it's off its highs it needs to go back down. This is what we call consolidation. The smart money is taking profits and churning individuals in and out of the stock while getting ready for the next leg up. Typically, if you are looking at the 1-minute chart, there is some confusion on this time frame, try looking at the 5 minutes to see what is going on there this will typically give you a better idea of what the stock/ticker is currently doing. Churning individuals in and out of the stock is not an uncommon thing. The smart money is trying to get everyone going in the same direction before pushing it the other way. This also holds for breakouts as well. The lower high here is the confirmation of the trend that you are looking for to the downside. This is the type of picture-perfect high, low, lower high you are looking for. If you look at the chart you can see a huge resistance area that kept pushing the stock/ticker down and the support area that needed to break was the New Low identified on the chart or the lower low. Once you have the lower high and the lower low breaks, you are in a confirmed downtrend and you can hold the trade. The area we identified as the entry point was on the lower high, out stop was tight here and we know what we were looking for in terms of the actual break here. The reason I identified this area as entry is because of the resistance area right above and how the stock/ticker backed off every single time. The entry that you should take would be the break of the "New Low" identified on the chart.

Trading is one of the most difficult things that I have undertaken, but it has also been the most rewarding. There is an enormous amount of freedom when trading. You get the feeling that you are on top of the world. Trading can bring you tons of great opportunities to see more things in life and to participate in what is really happening in the market. Your financial IQ will definitely increase because of the amount of detail that is needed to trade successfully. Although this may seem like a hard thing to do, I definitely think anyone with the discipline to follow directions and their own rules can make it trading. The 90% individuals that do not make it trading do not follow rules, do not have a set of rules to follow and are extremely undisciplined traders. The most important part of trading is to understand that losses are just the cost of doing business and they will happen. The successful trader knows this and welcomes small losses in search of the large gains. The best thing to do in trading is to continue to learn, take small losses so you are protecting your principal which will give you more time in the market and give you the opportunity to take advantage of the big trades that will increase your account along the way.

Chapter 5 - Planning Your Trade

Imagine wanting to design your own dream house. You're excited by all the possibilities, so you go to the store and start picking stuff out. You don't think you need a plan because it's all in your heart and mind so you pick out some lumber that could be useful, some furnishings that might be interesting and of course, pick out the curtains. As you start building your house, you realize that the wood you bought is wrong, and because of the timing, your furnishings and curtains won't work. You go back to the store and try again and again. You see pictures of houses you like and keep adding their features to your house. Much later, your house is finally built. It's a mix of a variety of features, and it's holding itself up. It's a house that you can probably sleep in, but it also costs you a lot of money, wasted materials, and time. Trading without having a plan is a lot like building a house without a plan. You can definitely make it work but it will cost you a lot of money, waste your trades, and your time.

We've kept harping on the importance of having strategies and plans. That's because this is a critical skill in trading. Trading isn't about following your gut decisions. Once you start doing that, then you've gotten into random gambling instead of trading with as much precision as you can.

A trading plan is vitally important, and each trader should have one. It's strongly recommended that you write your trading plan down. It can be digital or physical, but having a centralized area where you can write down your trading plan, strategies and goals can help you stay on track. This can also be the area where you write your trades and keep notes for future trades. Then, before and after every trade, evaluate your plan, add notes, and analyze your progress. To create your trading plan, start by analyzing your situation, finding your objectives and then make a trading plan.

Analyze your situation

Your trading plan should start with you understanding your situation. This goes hand in hand with the money management aspect of risk management. Understanding your situation means that you know exactly where you are financially, how much it costs to have an account for trading, and how much each trade will cost you. This means knowing which brokerage accounts you will trade out of, how much you can afford to keep in your account, how many trades you can afford in a week. All of this goes into analyzing your situation.

To find out this information, you'll have to do some research. You're already doing a great job by reading this book. But there's always more research to do. Look at the different trading firms you want to have an account in. What are their benefits or drawbacks? Do they have any incentives that might help you down the road?

Make sure you know their commission costs for trades, since this comes out of your profits. Check to see if they can accommodate options trading if that's the route you're going for.

Then look into your financials and be entirely honest with yourself. How much debt do you have? Are you willing to do minimum payments on your debts and put money towards investments? Or would you rather pay more of your debt and only use a small amount for trading? It's your choice, but the point is that you need to take a good long look at your finances before getting into trading and investing. Remember, while you'll gain some from trading, you'll also likely lose some. Therefore, if you're not in the right financial situation, then wait before you begin trading capital.

Once you've understood and analyzed your situation, it's time to set out your objectives for trading.

Find your objectives

Why do you want to swing trade? This is the first question you should ask yourself when making your trading plan. It can be the first thing you write down wherever you keep your plan. This way, every time you see it and you study the plan, you're reminded of why you're doing this. Don't just leave this question unanswered. This question is the basis of all of your trades and can be the motivation to continue trading, even after a loss. Once you've analyzed your motivations, it's time to look at your goals for trading. Is your goal to save up for something, to make an income, to experiment with trading, or to have extra funds for your daily life? Knowing your overall goal can help you to then determine how much you want to make in a year of trading. Then make smaller goals, moving down from the year.

All of your goals should be SMART goals. These goals are:

- Specific
- Measurable
- Attainable
- Realistic
- Time-bound

Specific goals are ones where you know the endpoint. A goal, for example, might be, "I want to have extra money in my account so that I can enjoy my hobby of competitive polo." Or it can be something like "I want to buy a house." While these goals are good, they're not specific enough. Try to consider things like timeline, who is helping with the goal, amount needed, and how it will be achieved. To remake the first example goal, you might say: "I want to swing trade to make $200 extra dollars to spend each month so that I can buy a horse for competitive polo by the end of the year." That is a specific goal. Now you need to determine how you will measure success towards your goal.

Measurable goals are ones that you can easily evaluate. It's basically proof that you are meeting your goal. Your measure may be seeing money in your bank account, but that's pretty vague. List a specific amount you want to see each week in your account, or state what percentage you would like to make in trades. You can also see each successful trade as a measure of reaching your goal. So long as you have a clear set of numbers to assess, then you have a measurable goal because they can easily be seen and recorded. Then you'll know whether you are on track with your goal. If you're not on track, then you may need to reevaluate your process or the timeline for the goal.

Attainable goals are reachable based on how much time you have available, how much effort you put in, and the resources available to you. If your goal is to make one million dollars in a year by swing trading, you have to analyze whether or not that is attainable. Do you have the necessary funds and time to dedicate to that much trading? Do you have the knowledge that you'll need in order to make that much? Having attainable goals means that they fit into what you are capable of doing right now. If you don't have the funds, time, energy, or experience to put towards the goal, then your goal needs to be more attainable based on your current life skills and style.

Realistic goals are ones that you are actually capable of achieving. This goes hand in hand with attainable goals. Realistic goals are ones that you are capable of achieving and are relevant to you. If you know there might be a lack in an aspect of your goal, then a realistic goal includes the steps you need to take to fix it. For example, if your goal is to successfully trade by writing options, but you don't know the first thing about writing options, then this goal is not realistic. Instead, it's better to start with the goal of learning how to write options. Realistic goals need to be ones that you can honestly reach, not ones that are sky-high. Otherwise, you're just setting yourself up for disappointment.

Time-bound goals are ones that have a very specific deadline, or multiple deadlines. If you don't have a deadline for your goal, then you may not actually work towards it. It's like writing a paper for school. If your teacher says you can turn it in whenever it's very likely it will never be turned in. But if you have a specific time that paper needs to be turned in, then you'll work hard to get it finished in time. You want to do the same with your goals. Make time goals, or specific deadlines you would like to meet to ensure that you are actually progressing. How you measure the time is up to you. A lot of people use physical graphs they can chart to show that they're meeting their timing goals. This way, it's something you have to do on paper, and something you can keep in a convenient place like your bathroom mirror, or fridge. Having a physical time tracker can be really lovely because you can see your success right there in front of you. You can also add it to your trading plan so that at the end of the goal, when you've reached it, you can go back and re assess your progress. Either way, having some time-bound goals will make reaching your goals easier and give you a sense of satisfaction when you make it before your deadlines.

All of these steps are what make good goals, great. However, sometimes the goal doesn't work out and it needs to be reevaluated. Reevaluating your goal is not a negative thing, it just means that you need to clarify it, find out what to change, and adapt your goal into a smarter one. When you've made your goals as clear as possible, then you're put on a road to successfully completing your goals.

Once you have chosen your goals for swing trading, it's time to get down to brass tacks and create your investment plan.

Chapter 6 - Daily Routine of a Swing Trader

Swing traders differ from investors in various ways. Investors buy shares and hold on to them for lengthy periods of time. They often hope to generate annual returns, like 10% to 20% per annum on their investments. This is a different approach from traders who enter the markets and exit after a very short while. Traders hope to make small but frequent profits in the course of a few days or weeks. Their aim is to make between 10%–15% or more each month. This translates into big returns over time.

Swing traders use both fundamental analysis and technical analysis to determine stocks with an upward trend and with momentum. A swing trader's work includes the identification of financial instruments such as stocks that have a well-defined trend.

The aim of a swing trader is to purchase securities when the prices are low, hold the securities for a couple of days, and then exit when the prices are high. This way, they exit trades profitably, and it is the method that they use to earn their profits. It makes sense to enter trades when prices are low and then sell when the prices go up.

As a retail trader, you may be at a disadvantage compared to professional traders. Professional traders are generally more experienced, have a lot of leverage, access to more information, and pay lower commissions. However, you do have some advantages in some instances because you are not limited to the risks that you can take, size of investment, and types of trades. As a retail swing trader, you need to ensure that you have all the knowledge necessary to take full advantage of the markets.

Trading Techniques

Swing trading techniques are easy to learn. They are also straightforward and simple to demonstrate. After learning these techniques, it is advisable to put them to practice for a couple of days until you get confident enough to trade live. If your practice trades were largely successful, then trading the real markets will also likely prove to be successful.

As a swing trader, you do not have to focus your energies using complicated formulas and learning complex techniques. You also do not need to buy and hold stocks or other financial instruments like currencies. Instead, you only need your trading charts.

Beginning of the Trading Day

As a swing trader, you need to be up early before the markets open. Most traders are awake by 6.00 in the morning and start preparing for their trading day. The few moments just before the opening of the markets are crucial as you get the feel of the market.

One of the first things that you need to focus on is finding a potential trade. You should spend your time finding securities that are on a sure trend. Another thing you should focus during these early morning moments is creating a watch list of stocks and securities. Also, check out all your other positions.

Current News and Developments

You should take time in the morning to catch up with the latest developments and news, especially those that directly impact businesses. One of the best sources of financial and business news is CNBC, which is a cable news channel.

As a swing trader, you need to be on the lookout for three things in the news. These are different sentiments in various market sectors, current news reports such as earnings reports, and the overall market outlook. Are there sectors that are in the news? Is the news considered good or bad? What significant thing is happening in other sectors? If something significant or of concern happens, then you are likely to come across it in the news.

Identifying Potential Trades

So how do you find trades that you'd be interested in? As a swing trader, you may want to find a catalyst. A fundamental catalyst will enable you to enter a trade with sufficient momentum. Then all you will need is technical analysis to confirm your exit and profit points.

1. Special Opportunities

There are different ways of entering the market. One of these is to find a great opportunity with so much potential. Great opportunities can be found through companies planning an IPO, those ready to file for bankruptcy, situations of takeovers, buyouts, insider buying, mergers, acquisitions, and restructuring. These and other similar events provide excellent trading opportunities, especially for swing traders.

To find these opportunities, you need to check out the SEC website or filings from companies. Certain forms such as 13-D and S-4 contain all the relevant information that you need. While these opportunities carry some inherent risks, the possible rewards are too great to ignore.

2. Sector or Industry Opportunities

Apart from the rare opportunities, we also have opportunities that are specific to a given sector. These are opportunities that you will find on certain websites regarding sectors whose performance is well above average. For instance, we can determine that sectors such as energy are doing exceptionally well by observing energy ETFs. There are certain sectors that pose a high risk but have high returns and can be very profitable.

3. Chart Breaks

We can also rely on chart breaks to find opportunity. Chart breaks are especially suitable for swing traders. Chart breaks are really Stocks or securities that have been traded so heavily such that they are very close to major resistance or support levels. As a swing trader, you will search for opportunities out there by identifying patterns indicating breakdowns or breakouts.

These identifying patterns can be Gann or Fibonacci levels, Wolfe Waves, channels, and triangles. However, please note that these chart breaks are only useful when there is huge interest in the stock. This way, you can easily enter and exit trades. Therefore, whenever you note this chart breaks, you should also focus on factors such as price and volumes.

Securities Watch List

One of the things that you really should embark on is building a list of stocks or other securities to watch closely. The stocks that should constitute this list include those with a great chance at high volumes and upward price movement. It should also include stocks with a major catalyst.

Checking Your Current Positions

It is important to keep tabs on your current positions. You probably have other trades so take a look at these and see if there is anything needed on your part. This is something that you should focus on early before the trading day begins. You should double check these positions with the benefit of foresight based on the information obtained from news sources and online sites. See if any news items will affect your current positions.

Checking this out is pretty easy and straightforward. All that you need to do is to enter the stock symbol into websites. This will reveal plenty of essential information that you need to be successful. Should you come across any material information that can directly affect your trades, then consider what you should do, such as adjusting the different points like take profit and stop loss.

Market Hours

Now that the markets are open, it is time to get busy as a trader. During this time, you will mostly be trading and watching your screen. Check the market makers of the day and also be aware of any fake bids and asks.

Find a viable trade and apply all the skills and knowledge you have acquired to identify entry and exit points. There are plenty of techniques you can apply to arrive at these points. Think about Fibonacci extensions, for example. These can help you identify entry and exit points; you can also use price by volume and resistance levels.

As the trading day proceeds, you may need to make certain adjustments to your positions. These adjustments will depend on a number of factors. However, it is not advisable to adjust positions once you enter a trade, especially if you are planning on taking on additional risks. If you have to make adjustments, then it is better to focus more on adjusting the take profit points and stop-loss levels.

After Hours

Most swing traders are largely inactive after the normal trading day is over. At this point in time, the market is not liquid at all and the available spread not suitable to enter any trades. Therefore, take this time to do some evaluation of your earlier trades and your positions. Examine your trades and see where you could do better. Focus on any open positions you may have and consider all material events that could have some effect on your positions.

To be an efficient trader, you need to have a routine. You should learn to wake up early before the beginning of the trading day and to get prepared. You also need to automate as many processes as possible. The crucial step is learning how to set up your workstation and your trading computer. Doing this ensures that you are totally ready for the trading day.

As a trader, you really need to learn how to separate charting from trading. There needs to be a different platform for charting. It is just when you are ready to begin trading that you will log onto your trading platform.

There is a good reason for this. If you use the same platform for both charting and trading, you may fall into the trap of impulse decision. You will clearly view your orders right in front of your face. This will create a sense of panic and urgency, and you may do things in a hurry. When they are on different platforms, you create a thin layer that prevents impulsive action.

It is advisable to learn how to use templates a lot more effectively. This helps, especially with the charting. Charting becomes an extremely effective and efficient process when you come up with different templates with varying colors. For instance, you can come up with a different color for resistance and support levels and other tools. The next time that you trade, it will be easy to track each tool individually based on its color code.

You can use the weekends to plan the coming trading week. You can do this without the worry or concern of active markets. You can also take the time to come up with different trading strategies and styles that can help you attain your trading goals.

Think up of different situations that can arise as you trade and then come up with suitable solutions for each. This way, should any situation happen in the course of the trading week, then you will be well prepared to handle it. Sometimes, though, you may feel the need to use a trading template already designed. These can be found online and are easy to download. However, you can also come up with your own trading plan and strategy to implement. In brief, you should always enter a trade with a plan in hand. This means that you should plan your trade and then trade your plan.

Chapter 7 - Entry and Exit Strategies for Traders

The most obvious entry and exit strategy that exists in trades is to buy low and sell high, but there is more to having a strong entry and exit strategy than just that if you are going to earn a profit from your trades. Ultimately, your entry and exit strategies are the most important parts of your deal as they give you the best opportunity to earn the most profit off of every single deal that you become invested in.

The best strategy that you can use to help you choose when to make trade deals is to follow the candles in your trading platform. On your trading platform, when you open the proper tab to open the market trends for any given stock, you are going to see what are known as candles, which are the ticks that indicate what the market was doing, and how much of it was being done, at any given time. The larger the candle the more momentum came behind that move, the smaller the candle the less momentum came behind that move. Larger candles indicate that the trend is going to be more consistent and intense in any given direction, whereas smaller candles indicate that it is going to be less consistent and likely less intense in that given direction. While this is not always the case, it is generally the best way to follow the market. With that being said, be wary of larger candles as they can indicate an overcorrection in the market which may be rapidly followed by a switch in the opposite direction.

Choosing your entry and exit strategies come from looking for where the exact swings are happening in the market, and how they are determined by the candles. You want to read the swing point lows by paying attention to where the market dips and following the three candles around that dip that are larger, smaller, and then larger again. Although the smallest one may not be at the lowest dip of the market, they are an indication that the market direction is about to swing into the opposite direction virtually every single time. Ideally, you should be buying into your market as soon as you see this swing take place between three candles.

When it comes time to exit the market, or sell your stocks, you want to watch for the same sort of trend happening in the opposite direction. In this case, you will see swing point highs at the top of the market where the market is starting to peak right before swinging back into a downtrend direction. These swing point highs are indicated by three candles that are generally indicated by one candle being quite large, another being smaller, and then an even smaller candle. When you see the candles starting to get smaller, you know that they are indicating a loss in momentum and the trend is starting to switch out of favor. This would ideally be when you would sell your stocks so that you do not endure the downtrend, or the switch that would result in you losing out on your profits from that trade.

It is important to understand that not every swing is going to create a powerful reversal in the market, but it can indicate that one is about to start. A reversal will never happen without a swing point developing, so you need to be aware of these and pay attention to when and how they are developing in the market. It can be helpful for you to start monitoring these and paying attention to how they look and what they create before you start making trades, in order to have money invested you know exactly what you are looking for. This may help you make a more confident and logical trade move, rather than an emotional one caused by fear of the market changing directions.

71

Chapter 8 - Protecting Your Capital and Managing Your Money

Your mindset provides you with a strong opportunity to hedge yourself against risk in your trades, but it is not the only way that you can protect yourself. You also need to make sure that you are protecting yourself in practical ways against risks in the market so that you are taking advantage of all the tools available to help you succeed.

When it comes to trading, you can never be too careful and you should always be exercising every technique possible to protect yourself against risks in the market.

Protecting Through Diversifying

One of the best things you can do to protect yourself when you are trading is to diversify your portfolio. Diversifying your portfolio means that you are investing your capital into multiple trade deals so that you are invested in several areas. The reason why diversification hedges you against risk is that it prevents you from the likelihood of total losses.

In this case, if one of your trades does not perform well, another one of your trades is likely to outperform it and make up for that loss. As long as you are doing your best to research every single trade and trade with confidence, you are likely to see success in many of your trades if you use this strategy, and the losses you do see will not be nearly as catastrophic.

People who want to earn a serious profit with trading are virtually always invested in multiple deals at once to ensure their success, as this increases your potential for maximizing profits, as well.

When it comes to diversifying, there are three ways that you can do it. The first way is to become involved in multiple trade deals that are all fairly similar in nature, for example, getting involved in multiple different options trades.

If you are brand new to trading, it is advisable that you use this diversification style first and that you master trading options before you move on to any other form of investing or trading. This way, you are able to develop your confidence and skill in options first before venturing off into a new trading strategy.

The other two types of diversification that you can engage in with trades include diversifying with non-correlating assets and diversifying your risk category. Both of these are going to help you limit your risk while also improving your money management skills, which will ultimately help you become a smart and successful trader.

Diversifying with Non-Correlating Assets

Diversifying with non-correlating assets is a strategy that you can execute almost right away when you begin trading options. The key to this diversification is that the underlying assets that you are trading are different from all of your trades. For example, some of your trades may involve assets such as bonds and ETFs, whereas others might include commodities and currencies.

By changing the underlying assets that are being traded, you hedge yourself not only against fluctuations in the specific stock that you are investing in but also in the industry that this stock is a part of. In this case, if the industry itself takes a hit, you are not at risk of having every single trade deal you have made suffer due to it. Instead, you can feel confident that a strong portion of your portfolio remains unhindered from that fluctuation and you have no reason to panic.

If you want to take this a step further, after you have grown confident in options, you can begin to diversify your trading style by investing some of your funds elsewhere.

I will not elaborate too much into this as it is not relevant to swing trading with options, however, do understand that it can protect you in your investment portfolio overall while also giving you the greatest earning potential with your capital.

Diversifying Your Risk Category

The other way that you can and should diversify your portfolio is by diversifying your risk category. When it comes to trading, there are three risk categories that you can fall into including conservative, moderate, and high. Conservative trades allow you to guarantee a profit from your gains, however, the amount being guaranteed is often very small and does not generally have room for significant growth.

Moderate trades do carry a higher risk with them; however, they also earn you bigger profits in the long run. If you trade moderately, a strong trading strategy can help you succeed with those trades which will increase your chances of securing your profits. High-risk category trades are those that have a high potential to fail, but if they do succeed, they will carry massive profits with them. These tend to be the most stressful investments because of how large the risk is, but if they go through the returns, you get can be huge.

Generally, every trader has a risk category that they tend to stick to with most of their trades. This category will likely fluctuate as they grow older, as the older you get, the more you are going to need to have your profits available for you to use, and the less time you will have to recover from any losses you incur in your trades. For this reason, it is advised that you actually use your age to help you determine what risk category you should be trading with when you are making trades.

75

The easiest way to determine your category is to subtract your age from 100. The value of your age should be the percentage of your funds invested into conservative investments, whereas the value remaining is free to be invested in moderate or high-risk investments. Ideally, you should further apply this rule to decide which percentage should be invested in moderate risk versus which should be invested in high risk, so that your money is always being invested in a way that is appropriate for your age.

For example, if you are 25, then 25% of your overall investment capital should be invested in conservative investments. Then, 25% of your remaining investment capital should be invested in moderate investments, with your other 75% being invested in high-risk investments.

If you are 60, then 60% of your overall investment capital should be invested in conservative profiles, and 60% of your remaining investment capital should be invested in moderate investments, and the rest can be invested in high-risk investments. You can always adapt your chosen strategy based on what you feel your needs are and what level of risk you are willing to incur, but using this as a guideline is a great way to ensure that you are managing your money properly.

This way, you are able to maximize your profits while also ensuring that the capital you need will be accessible when you need it at any period in your life.

The 2% Rule of Money Management

In addition to ensuring that your portfolio is diversified with different investments and risk categories, you also want to make sure that you are managing your capital with each individual trade that you make. Ideally, you should never be trading more than 2% of your overall investment capital into any single trade. So, if you have 5000 to invest, you should never be investing more than $100 into any given bare-bones.

This ensures that you are diversifying your portfolio enough to protect yourself against risks while also increasing your likelihood of gaining profits from each trade. If you trade more than 2% of your investment capital into any given risk, you massively expose yourself to losses that can devastate your portfolio and your investments.

Realizing this rule and putting it to work in your own trading portfolio might seem overwhelming early on when you are brand new to trading. You might find yourself concerned that you will not be able to effectively manage all 50 trades, which is a reasonable fear when it comes to starting out as a trader. Understand that enacting this rule does not mean that you are obligated to get started in 50 different trades all at once, effectively overwhelming yourself with attempting to manage them all.

Instead, you can start with managing just 1 trade, and then increase to managing 3-5 trades, and then continue increasing until all of your investment capital is sunk into different investments.

Gradually increasing the number of trades, you are involved in will not only help you grow used to managing all of these trades, but it will also prevent you from becoming fearful or overwhelmed and making emotional trade deals. Early on, it is perfectly okay to start small and build your way up as your confidence grows, as this can be a powerful opportunity to increase your success in trades.

The 5% Risk Account

Some people think that a trade deal should only include the capital that was required to buy into that trade deal, including the cost per share and the commissions that you pay to the brokerage to make your deal. While it is true that this is the only money you require to get involved in a trade, it is not true that it is the only amount that you should set aside for a trade.

If you want to manage your money effectively and hedge yourself against risk, you should always invest 5% of a total investment amount into a "risk account." This account ensures that you have enough capital to recover the losses should one occur, enabling you to carry on trading. Without it, you might find that some of your losses have catastrophic impacts on your bottom line and significantly reduce the number of trades you can afford to actively engage in, which directly damages your profitability.

Keeping that risk account open with 5% of your total investment capital (or more if you are engaging in riskier trades) will ensure that you are protected and that you can continue to make trades even if you experience a loss.

Conclusion

In the end, though, swing trading may not be for everyone. So do not get depressed if it does not work out for you. Along the way, however, something to consider is applying swing trading in different markets if you find that your first stab at it does not work. One thing that I know was going to happen is a lot of people are going to be interested in swing trading on Forex. For some reason, the currency exchange market holds a lot of appeal for a lot of people. And that is fine as far as it goes. Many people are actually pretty successful on the market. At the same time a lot of people or not, because that is a really touchy market. So, my advice if you decide to start off trading Forex, and it does not work out for you, is that you should not give up on swing trading altogether. Instead, try regrouping and then, even though it is not quite as exciting, try swing-trading stocks instead.

The same problem might arise when it comes to trading options. I have a lot of experience trading options. While I have had a lot of fun doing it, you need to be aware if you have not tried it yet, that trading options can be very tricky. It is also something that gives you the opportunity on a bad day to watch your money melt away. Options are very sensitive to price changes in the underlying stock. This can range from a 50% to 100% proportional change. So, what this means is that if the stock rises or falls by a dollar, the price of your option could rise or fall anywhere from $50-$100. An expensive stock says over $200, is not going to be a stock that is undergoing a significant change from a dollar drop in the price. So, you can see that options can be a security that magnifies both gains and losses. The upshot of this is that options trading is not for the thin-skinned. Something else to consider is that options are actually a little bit complicated. Some new traders who may be intrigued by the idea might not really understand what they are doing and they might get themselves into trouble as a result.

Note that if you start off trading options, and you find that it is not working out, that is not necessarily a reason to give up swing trading. Again, what I would recommend it if you follow this path and that happen is you should consider dropping options but continuing swing trading would something simple like stocks.

People might be put off by the higher price of stocks, but you can start off small and working way up with time. Do not start off thinking about trading 50 or 100 shares at a time. To learn the ropes, you can even start off only trading a single share if that is all you can afford. Even though that is not something that is going to make you any significant money, it would serve as a great training ground, and you would learn how to enter and that your position at the right times. It would also provide a way for you to learn how to do your technical analysis on the real data without really having much risk on the line. Then, as time goes on, you can increase the number of shares that you are trading until you get to the point where you are making real money.

Another thing to say is that you should not jump off a cliff. And what I mean by this, is that you should not quit your job or take other radical actions right away in order to swing trade. In the beginning, at least when you are a swing trading stocks or Forex, you can certainly do it on a part-time basis. It is not necessary to sit at the computer all day long the way that a day trader has to do.

CPSIA information can be obtained
at www.ICGtesting.com
Printed in the USA
LVHW051412250621
691051LV00005B/426